Below the Green Pond

Paul Humphrey

Illustrated by
Carolyn Scrace

Evans

Let's look at the pond.

What's all that green stuff on the top?

That's duckweed. Look! Over there is a waterlily and there's a heron, looking for fish.

4

What other animals can you see?

Ducks and coots.

It's fun looking at the surface of the pond, but what happens under water is even more exciting. Let's take a look.

See how they have webs between their toes to help them move faster?

8

What's that jelly stuff over there?

They are frogs' eggs, which are called frog-spawn.

Can you see the black dots in the jelly?

They're the eggs and some of them have hatched out.

Do you know what those wriggly things are called?

Tadpoles.

10

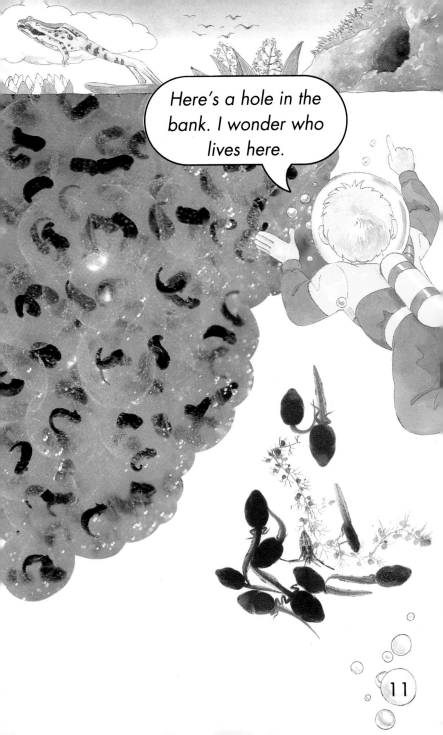

Wrong. It's a water vole.
It is different from a rat.

These animals are great, but some of the smaller ones are even more interesting. Let's shrink down to their size and take a look. But be careful.

Wow! This is scarey! Look at that huge fish over there.

14

Pike

Trout

It's not really huge. It's just that you are small. Now you know what it is like to be as tiny as an insect.

15

Here's some more jelly. Is that frog-spawn too?

No. Those are the eggs of the greater
pond snail. The shell of the greater
pond snail can be up to 5
centimetres long!

Look! What is happening here?

This spiny male stickleback has made a nest. Now he is 'dancing' to attract a female. She will lay her eggs in the nest but then the male looks after them.

He has very bright colours.

Those make him look handsome to a female.

This newt will eat the tadpoles and baby sticklebacks if he gets a chance.

Look at his spines.
He looks like a stegosaurus.

He is called a great crested newt.

21

23

Look at this great diving beetle. It has caught a stickleback.

24

Now we're going to shrink down even smaller and look at things that you can't usually see.

These creatures are really weird. What are they?

They are Cyclops and Daphnia. They are so small that you need a magnifying glass to see them properly.

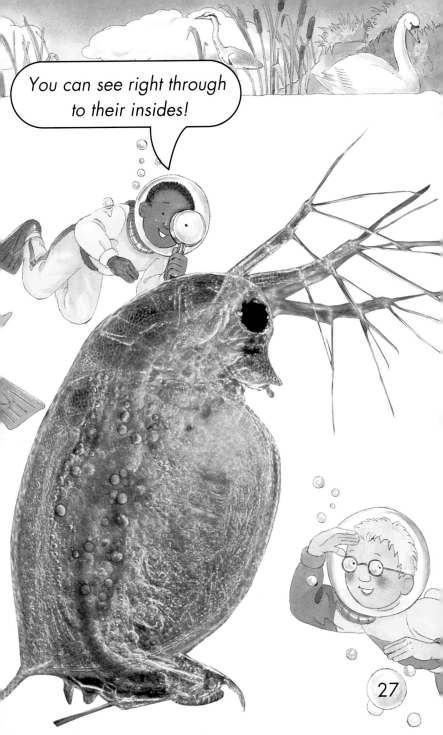

Look at the picture. How many of the
animals and plants can you name?
The answers are on the next page but
don't peep until you have tried yourself.

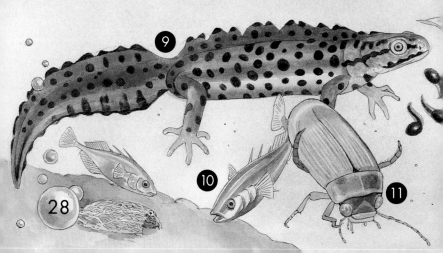

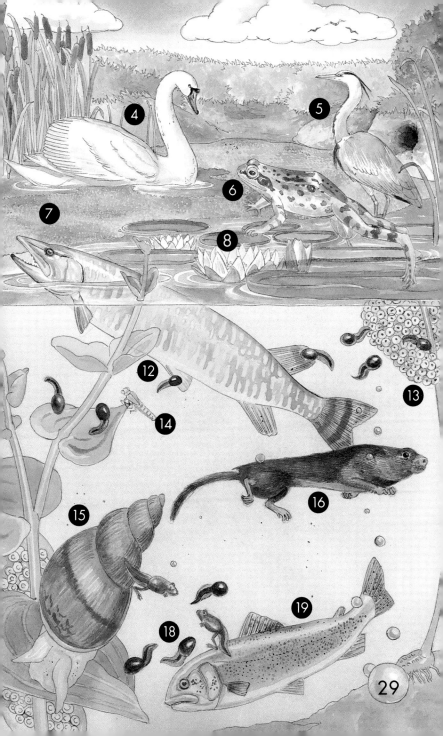

The photographs in this book show many animals much bigger than their real sizes. This is how big the animals really are compared to you.

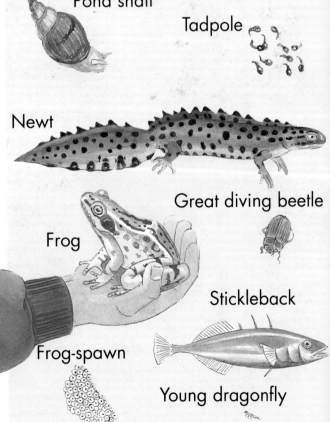

Pond snail

Tadpole

Newt

Great diving beetle

Frog

Stickleback

Frog-spawn

Young dragonfly

30